# The Path of Forgetting

## The Microcosm In the Macrocosm

# The Path
# of Forgetting

## The Microcosm
## In the Macrocosm

*Gabriele*

Gabriele
Publishing House

Second Edition, December 2016
Published by:
© Gabriele Publishing House
Max-Braun-Str. 2
97828 Marktheidenfeld, Germany

Tanslated from the original German title:
"Der Weg des Vergessens
Der Mikrokosmos im Makrokosmos"

Order No. S 348ENPOD
The German edition is the work of reference for all
questions regarding the meaning of the contents



ISBN 978-3-89201-807-0

# Table of Contents

We truly are living in a time that has never existed, neither before nor after the time on Earth of Jesus, the Christ. The Spirit of God, who is calling to each of His children, pours out His word of truth in a fullness never before known. Thus, it is possible for every person, for every soul, to take the path back to the Father's house, which is taught in all detail.

This could only happen because, during this time, a messenger of light in the earthly garment is available to Him and directly conveys the word of God. Beyond that, the messenger of light shows every willing contemporary person the path to freedom, simultaneously pointing out the steps that lead to the expansion of consciousness. It is Gabriele, the great prophetess of God, who, for over 35 years, has untiringly served Him and her fellow people, her brothers and sisters.

In this book by Gabriele, we are given an understanding of the great cosmic correlations from the source of divine love and wisdom – and particularly, the significance of these iron-clad principles of the law for the life of each individual person, each individual soul. Anyone who delves into these and grasps the content more and more will certainly treat his life – all life – more cautiously and consciously.

*Gabriele Publishing House*

## Introduction

In this book, we are introduced in a unique way to the inherent laws of life, which open up a new dimension of existence to us. Universal correlations between the microcosm and the macrocosm are explained in such a way that they encompassingly convey the lawful processes that are at the basis of all life. New recognitions, whose far-reaching significance for how one lives one's life are of inexpressible value, will open up to the one who not only reads this book, but reflects on it and relates it to all that he, as an individual, encounters at every moment.

We learn how everything that we feel, think, say and do as human beings is not only continuously stored in the microcosm man, but is in constant communication with further memory sources in the coarse-material macrocosm and beyond that, in a finer-material macrocosm.

Modern science is also making use of the knowledge about storage capacities, communication and the law of sending and receiving.

As never before in the history of mankind, modern science avails itself of a resource that is based on a coarse replica, a utilization of cosmic laws that have been turned into their opposite. The Internet offers astral possibilities, which partially open up abysmal depths. In the Internet area, many a user creates artificial worlds for himself, into which he enters, in order to lead a kind of equivocal second life, not belonging to him, in the virtual world of imagination.

In these virtual worlds, people delude themselves with an imaginary, but for them new, personality profile, a new identity, which does not fit with their actual human identity. They fashion and store a desired constellation of traits and characteristics of a virtual personality, through which they then move, through which they communicate and act, as they would in their physical life. All their movements, all their communications, all that is successively built up and constantly expanded upon, is minutely stored in the gigantic storage system of the Internet. Every movement leaves behind traces, which at any time allow inferences about the author, who stored the content in the network.

In this way, a gigantic communication and data network develops, which is connected with each other and in which networks of relationships of virtual persons are formed, who operate, move, communicate and act in it, just as takes place in the material world. As real as it seems to the users, for straightforward thinking people it should be clear that this illusory world is unreal and will sooner or later lead to severe complications, because it has been inverted into what is contrary to the present personal human life. It excludes communication with the identity brought by the soul. Permit me to say: The virtual pattern is the dregs of Satan. Our world is similarly made for those people who do not know themselves.

Only the fewest people know who they are, not to mention where they come from and where they are going. Most people live their life in the illusory world of matter, as if it were the sole reality.

The well-known physics professor Hans-Peter Dürr once said: "Matter is like the dross of the Spirit." Physics knows that matter is merely an energetic phenomenon; it is energetic structures that are subject to transformation just as we can observe it in all life forms. Matter is not everlasting. A person who assumes it to be the sole reality is passing by his true life.

Just as the virtual world can be called up in the Internet by the astral side, so does that person become a plaything of contrary forces, who takes each day as it comes, who lets himself drift and does not recognize who he himself is.

Do you know, do we know, who we are?

Many a one takes each day as it comes, often not knowing what is going on behind his feelings and thoughts, and thus, with whom he comes into communication and contact. Many people talk, but they do not figure out which feelings and thoughts they are having at the same time. They act, but often do not recognize their deeper motives.

But even though we do not know it – everything is stored and recorded. Where? Among other places, in the stars.

The stars do not accuse. They point out. The truth about each one of us lies in the stars. The stars know each one of us utterly and completely; we are like an open book to them. Do we also know ourselves? Are we an open book for ourselves? If yes, then we don't need the virtual, the astral, world. The stars see through us! Do we see through ourselves, each one, himself?

We can't pretend anything to the stars, for instance, when we pretend to be magnanimous or modest, a good donor or a good monarch. We can pretend many things to people. However, the stars reveal our masks and our masquerades to us, for the stars do not lie. It will be bitter for many to someday have to look at themselves, warts and all, be it as human being or as soul. Even though on this side of life we may act ever so patronizing, ever so magnanimously – it is possible that as a soul we'll arrive in the beyond as an imposter, when the masks come off; for the satanic is an impostor and many a one falls for this.

However, the bookkeeping of the All-consciousness, of the cosmic Being, is precise and just.

Everything that is described in this book is real. Whether we want to accept it or not, whether we think about it or not, whether we push it aside and dismiss it or not – everyone will one day experience it, at the latest, when he closes his physical eyes and recognizes that behind the life on Earth, which seemed so real to him, another reality is at work. At the latest, this reality opens to each soul when, step by step, it recognizes and clears up the inputs, or causes, that its person created, that is, when it surrenders them to cosmic transformation. On the path of forgetting, it thus grows into the inherent laws of life that correspond to the sole reality, the eternal homeland of our true Being.

*Martin Kübli*

*No energy is lost –
Where does it go?*

The "Path of Forgetting" – an engrossing topic, because no one is excluded, when it is: "The microcosm in the macrocosm."

A few questions to start with:
Every person has his own personal past. If we think about our past, we realize that we can no longer remember a lot of details. We say so casually, "Well, what's past is forgotten." But since no energy is ever lost, where did the energies go? – for example, our feelings, sensations, thoughts, words, all the positive and negative in our life, also our habits, thus, all of our behavior patterns, everything that we categorize as "forgotten" or "over with"?

Often, we shrug off as trifling the question of whether the people we have insulted or even harmed have forgiven us or may still be suffering from it. But what has not been rectified, that is, forgiven, continues to exist, even if we have forgotten such unresolved situations. We people brush aside the factor "energy" all too lightly, but every energy that each one of us emits continues to exist; it is recorded in us, in the microcosm and in the macrocosm.

People who, for example, have a difficult time overcoming a blow of fate, often hear the following adage from acquaintances: "Time heals many wounds!" –
Yes, that's true, but only when we have left behind no wounds, no debt.

Jesus of Nazareth taught the following to the people of all generations:
*Settle matters quickly with your adversary who is taking you to court. Do it while you are still with him on the way, or he may hand you over to the judge, and the judge may hand you over to the officer, and you may be thrown into prison.*
"Or he may hand you over to the judge" – who is the judge? It is always the law of sowing and reaping.
"... and the judge may hand you over to the officer" – We ourselves are the officer; we

input our causes into our body and into our soul. This can be like a prison for us when the causes come into effect.

Science teaches us, and because science teaches it, many people start from the premise that everything is energy and that no energy is lost! If no energy is lost, where do the differing degrees of vibration of the energies remain? Where are they recorded? A comment from many people could be: "Well, you can't remember every little thing, all the details or situations with others! Who can?!" That's right: Who can? But each one of us has different occurrences in our memory, for example, certain situations, which led to disagreeable quarrels with our neighbor, often merely trifling things, which, however, have not been rectified. Or, incidents occur to us, which moved us in our thoughts for a long time, which we every now and then talked about with our friends and acquaintances. Or, altercations come to mind that we formerly had with our colleagues at work. And much more.

Many a thing has disappeared from view with a change of location. We moved to another city and, in this way, it appeared that we left behind all dissension and strife, often over useless concerns. Those who moved away were mostly all-too-happy to forget what the affected neighbor or colleague at work might have thought, whether he was able to cope with what had led to the dissensions, strife and accusations. – Many situations and incidents brought by daily life are, in general, too quickly shrugged off by the person with an aphorism like: "Out of sight – out of mind!" And yet, everything is energy. Where is the energy of all the excesses of the ego that were not rectified, paid off and expiated – since everything, but really everything, is energy?

It is similar with what lends us wings, for example, the exhilarating feeling to have graduated from high school with good grades, or the joy about a job that is offered to us and that we accepted – of course, with possibilities of advancement, whereby, today, at an advanced age, things go well for us. Another one perhaps basks in a variety of vacation memories, or he still extols the act of providence that brought him together with people who brought him unexpected advantages for his further life on Earth, and much more. Every person has his past, and each one of us remembers what preoccupied us over a longer period of time – particularly what was useful and brought us advantages.

Whatever moved us greatly in the past, for example, joy, occupational advantages and incidents during vacations, but also anger, grief, suffering, bad luck – all of this and much more is a part of every individual's life on Earth. Deeply impressing and long-lasting incidents and situations thus stay in our memory and are often still present in us, particularly when we talk from time to time about what strongly marked our life on Earth. Even if we can't remember all the details of whatever we still have before us in images, nevertheless the total impression remains. What brought joy, but also what was not in order in our life and didn't particularly serve its purpose, stays recorded in us.

If everything is energy, then we are constantly developing more energies in us, which may turn into whole complexes, because we think or talk about the same things over and over again. For example, we can still vividly see the hefty arguments, a quarrel, which developed into enmity. To this very day, we can't forget it because we are of the opinion that it was the other's fault and he is unwilling to reconcile.

All in all, we can say that we primarily remember those things that may very well be engraved in our level of feelings, and yet are still in our active consciousness, that is to say, those things to which we emotionally reacted, joyfully, but also irascibly angry, and which move us from time to time. In any case, we were a part of the pros and cons of the situation, and still are until today, because we produce energies with our thinking and speaking – that is, we react and act. We also stored energies when we were helpful and contributed to a good understanding. The same holds true when we were mean and nasty, above all, when our position was questioned in a particular case or issue.

*Every person is a microcosm
in the macrocosm –
we store and record unceasingly*

So if we assume that no energy is ever lost, then every situation and occurrence, all the pros and cons of our life on Earth are registered and stored – whether we can still remember each one or not. Everything, but truly everything that concerns us, shapes our consciousness. Our character develops from this, it imprints us and determines our thinking and acting. One wonders: Do all stirrings and inclinations, such as anger with others, all joys and sorrows, the bad and good luck, do they all stay with us as pictures? And where is it all stored, if no energy is ever lost?

Let us again realize that everything is energy. We think, think, talk, talk; we act and act – everything, but truly everything, is energy. It goes out from us, it comes into us and is stored. For this reason, the topic: The microcosm in the macrocosm. You, and all of us, are a microcosm. We store and record ourselves unceasingly in the planetary constellations of the material macrocosm and beyond that.

An example from modern technology makes it possible for us to be able to graphically relate to the following principles from the cosmic All-law, which is the inexhaustible, inviolable, unfathomable to us human beings, the eternally unchanging Spirit of infinity:

For many people, it has become a matter of course to let themselves be guided in their automobile by a navigation system. By simply inputting an optional goal, they trust that they will be safely guided by the navigation system to their goal. Once turning the navigation system on, the goal is defined and via the antenna of the vehicle, the system enters into communication with the corresponding satellites which, via the coordinates, at all times register and continuously follow the location of the vehicle and all its movements. With every movement, the satellites adjust themselves and store and evaluate the new data to suggest an updated travel plan based on the predefined programming.

This is made available to the driver. He orients himself to this and decides about his future route, about his speed, his breaks, detours, and much more. No matter where he is headed, regardless of which route he finally takes and at what speed he travels, the navigation system goes with him and always directly updates the exact location and altitude, the direction and speed of the vehicle. This entire network of communication projects the complete distance in all its details, from start to finish. At every moment, the communication between vehicle and satellites is given.

What to many people just a few decades ago was hardly imaginable has today become for many a daily matter of course. The navigation system with all its complex and technical functions of sending and receiving, of storing and coordinating, may be only a very coarse reflection of what takes place uninterruptedly between the microcosm, the human being, and the coarse material macrocosm. But it shows how precisely the sending and receiving, the storing and calling up of something is possible, even using technical means.

And for modern man, it has become something totally taken for granted that the satellites give detailed images of every corner of the Earth, in which everything is recorded: forests, fields, river courses, mountain ranges, lakes and seas, but also cities and towns. Everything, but really everything, is minutely recorded and stored in gigantic databases! Every change is documented; what crops a field produces, what streets are changed, how nature changes, how the glaciers are melting, etc., etc., etc. – everything is collected and continuously registered. As astonishing as all these technical achievements are for us human beings, when compared to the recording capacities and precision of the macrocosm, all this is only the most imperfect and primitive technology.

And how much more finely, every movement of every person and every facet of his sensations, feelings, thoughts, words and actions, are followed and registered by the macrocosm!

There, every, but really every change, be it ever so subtle, is perceived and updated accordingly.

Let us go back to further explanations of the universal cosmic principles of the law.

On a clear and starry night, let us look at the sky and ask: What is going on up there anyway? Let us allow a drop of heavenly knowledge to move our mind. The drop of heavenly wisdom states that you, every one of us, are a wholly individual, special microcosm in this material macrocosm, and beyond that, in a finer-material macrocosm, about which we will learn more.

Let us bring to mind that each one of us is a totally unique and specific microcosm that is connected to the visible macrocosm, the coarse-material cosmos, and that we are in communication with it and led by it – and moreover, with the invisible cosmoses.

The natural sciences usually assume that all sensations, thoughts and feelings are recorded in the brain. That if a person was to die and thus, his brain activity to cease, then accordingly, all the energy that he stored until this point would be deleted. But since no energy is lost, then after the demise of the physical body, the energy must be somewhere or other. The entire content of human sensing, feeling, thinking, speaking and acting is stored in the soul as energy. Every human being has a finer-material body, the soul, which can also be called the astral, or ether, body. Since no energy is lost, our soul continues to live after our physical death, namely, in the planetary constellations of a finer macrocosm.

What we have stored in our cells and thus, in our brain, as well, is also the engraving of our finer-material body, the soul. The soul's engraving is determined by each person himself through the abundance of his inputs during his life on Earth.

To repeat: Every decision, every situation, all thoughts, feelings, words, and actions determine our time on Earth. Whether we are for or against the cosmic All-Law – we store and record everything in the microcosm, that is, in ourselves, in our brain and in the organs of our physical body, and, at the same time, in our soul. This is the so-called engraving of the soul. This means that every fragment of a second of our life on Earth is stored as energy with its content.

Jesus, the Christ, revealed the following statements to us people:

*Are not two sparrows sold for a farthing? Yet none of them falls to the ground without the will of the Most High. Verily, even all the hairs on your head are numbered. Therefore, do not be afraid. If God cares for the sparrows, should He not care for you, too?*

And when each hair on our head is counted, as well as every sparrow that falls to the Earth, how much more, then, are our feelings, thoughts, words and actions counted – in the end, everything that we conceal behind what we merely pretend?

Who or what counts this? Often, they are amassed energies, clusters of stars, the collective fields of the same or similar degrees of vibration that count those things that are a part of us human beings, for example, the hairs on our head, or the sparrow that falls to the Earth. Everything is active energy that is not lost. Nothing disappears from the scene of life without a trace. Everything is followed, weighed, measured and registered.

It is the stars and planets of the material macrocosm and of the invisible macrocosm that are counting. They count and record only what every individual person places into his feelings, sensations, thoughts, words and actions, that is, what we conceal with our behavior patterns and do not want to disclose to others, all that which takes place on the quiet, as it were. All these processes are recorded as credits and debits in a precise bookkeeping of God, which will be further clarified.

All personal behavior patterns, all data and everything that seems important to us human beings is energy and is in communication with planetary constellations in the material cosmos and in the invisible macrocosm. All the stars and planets of the material cosmos and of the, for us invisible, finer-material macrocosm are repository planets. In these countless planetary constellations, they record the "for" and "against" of every single person.

The material cosmos is primarily the memory bank for the behavior of the human being, for his individual imprinting, that is, his appearance and his way of living. With grievous factors in a person's character, which mark the human appearance through his "for" and "against" in daily life, he builds in the macrocosm energy information that is close to the Earth, so-called matrixes for a possible future incarnation.

The finer-material macrocosm contains countless planetary constellations, purification spheres for souls. According to the engraving of a soul, according to the wrongdoings of its former person against the cosmic law of freedom and unity, they are the respective abodes of the soul.

All these inputs in the person and in his soul form the engraving, which, at the latest, after the demise of the person – that is, after the death of the body – take effect in the corresponding abodes of the soul, in the finer-material planetary constellations.

As already stated, the soul is a finer-material entity, a finer-material body, surrounded by garments of energy that reflect the burdens in differing shades of color, according to the engraving of the soul. Many people know about the so-called aura, also called corona, an aura that surrounds the person. At every moment, the aura changes its colors and movements according to the person's behavior patterns. Either it is emitting sparks or it is in balance, according to the content of the person's feelings, thoughts, words and actions. It is a constant movement of shades of color, which the person emits and which ultimately are a part of the soul.

What appears as the aura during an incarnation is referred to as the soul garments for the discarnate soul. So the garments of the soul are not created by a designer or tailor and are not sewn by a seamstress. The current prevailing radiation of its garments, which reflects its burdens, shows in its "garment," in the nuances of color of its aura. On the soul's journey, one energetic garment, one soul garment after the other comes into effect. This soul garment signals to the soul what presently needs to be recognized and cleared up, to be overcome, in the way of unlawful aspects.

During the course of clearing things up, like paying off the debt, that is, of working off what the person has encumbered his soul with, the garments of energy, the so-called soul garments, are transformed. If a soul strives more towards the light, the soul garments become finer and lighter. If the soul has paid off the debt it recognized, then the energy of this garment ray goes into the corresponding planetary constellation of the finer macrocosm. With the transformation of the negativity that once clung to it, the soul body that has become more light-filled has cleared up what related to this. The basely vibrating energy formations were transformed by the indwelling power of the cosmic Spirit in every soul, and, as stated, directed to the finer macrocosm. The forgetting of all that was still clinging to the soul begins at the moment the debt is being transformed into positive power.

The soul now radiates a finer, more light-filled garment and moves to higher, more light-filled planets, where it can recognize and pay off still more inputs recorded in its soul body. On its journey to ever finer energies of light, it is accompanied and advised by higher beings. Everything that still clings as negative aspects to the soul that has become more light-filled needs to be recognized and rectified.

After each phase of purification, which is the same as paying off a debt, these energies are transformed by the mighty eternal Spirit into that energy that is proper to the respective planetary constellation, which, for the time being, corresponds to the structure of the soul. What was all-too-human is discarded, overcome, and thus, forgotten. The soul continues step by step on the path of forgetting, until its soul-body has again taken on the radiation of its original, true being. The soul is then no longer a soul. It is the pure being, the spirit being, that has returned home to the Father's house, that has come back to the eternal homeland, to the Kingdom of God, to its infinitely eternal roots, to our infinitely eternal divine heritage.

## *"A Pilgrim Here I Wander"*

A hymn translated from German into English by Catherine Winkworth vividly outlines how the content and course of a person's life on Earth can look – a person who is aware of his journey toward God, the eternal primordial Intelligence, to his heavenly Father:

*A Pilgrim Here I Wander**

A pilgrim here I wander,
On earth have no abode,
My fatherland is yonder,
My home is with my God,
For here I journey to and fro,
There in eternal rest
Will God His gracious gift bestow
On all the toil-oppress'd.

---

* Chorale Book for England, Catherine Winkworth, 1863 (translated from Paul Gerhardt, "Ich bin ein Gast auf Erden, ("I Am A Guest on Earth") 1650), http://www.ccel.org/ccel/winkworth/chorales.pdf

For what hath life been giving,
From youth up till this day,
But constant toil and striving?
Far back as thought can stray,
How many a day of toil and care,
How many a night of tears,
Hath pass'd in grief that none could share,
In lonely anxious fears!

How many a storm hath lighten'd
And thunder'd round my path!
And winds and rains have frighten'd
My heart with fiercest wrath:
And cruel envy, hatred, scorn,
Have darken'd oft my lot,
And patiently reproach I've born,
Though I deserved it not.

Then through this life of dangers
I onward take my way;
But in this land of strangers
I do not think to stay.
Still forward on the road I fare
That leads me to my home,

My Father's comfort waits me there,
When I have overcome.

Ah yes, my home is yonder,
Where all the angelic bands
Praise Him with awe and wonder,
In whose Almighty hands
All things that are and shall be, lie,
By Him upholden still,
Who casteth down and lifts on high
At His most holy will.

That home have I desired,
'Tis there I would be gone;
Till I am well-nigh tired,
O'er the earth I've journey'd on;
The longer here I roam, I find
The less of real joy
That e'er could please or fill my mind,
For all hath some alloy.

The lodging is too cheerless,
The sorrow is too much;
Ah come, my heart is fearless,
Release it with Thy touch,

When Thy heart wills, and make an end
Of all this pilgrimage,
And with Thine arm and strength defend,
When foes against me rage.

Where now my spirit stayeth
Is not her true abode;
This earthly house decayeth,
And she will drop its load,
When comes the hour to leave beneath
What now I use and have;
And when I've yielded up my breath
Earth gives me but a grave,

But Thou, my Joy and Gladness,
O Thou, my Life and Light,
Wilt raise me from this sadness,
This long tempestuous night,
Into the perfect gladsome day,
Where bathed in joy divine,
Among Thy saints, and bright as they,
I too shall ever shine.

There shall I dwell for ever,
Not as a guest alone,

With those who cease there never
To worship at Thy throne;
There in my heritage I rest,
From baser things set free,
And join the chorus of the blest
For ever, Lord, to Thee.

Having arrived at the universal Being, in the eternal Father's house, nothing is foreign to the divine being. The spirit being is again among its brothers and sisters in the eternal Father's house. What once was – the all-too-human turbulences – has not only been discarded, but forgotten. It is as if this son, this daughter, of God, had never been away.

In the Kingdom of God there is no time, no yesterday, no today, no tomorrow, and thus, no transience. Everything is purest, clearest, finest energy, unity – the Being.

How did Jesus of Nazareth say it?:
*In my Father's house are many rooms; if it were not so, would I have told you, 'I am going there to prepare a place for you'?*

*The bookkeeping of God –
all details are registered,
all changes are updated*

Let's go back to the wandering soul: In both cosmoses – in the material cosmos as well as in the finer-material cosmos – all the behavior patterns of a person are registered, but every change is also updated and newly adjusted in its energy, according to the behavior of the individual. The complete person and soul – that is, all details – are recorded according to the absolutely just principle of "sending and receiving." And this takes place at every moment because the registry is just. And, as already indicated, these memory sources are also called the bookkeeping of the cosmoses, or the bookkeeping of God.

Let us realize once more that the material macrocosm primarily records the workings of the person in the three dimensions, that is, everything that the person needs in the three-dimensional world for his existence on Earth

– what corresponds to the human needs, and thus, everything that is a part of the human being in the material world. The programs for existence in a human life are the necessary "equipment," so to speak, to be able to function during the incarnation of the soul. So, it is all those things that we do as a matter of course each day, because it's just the way it is – for example, opening doors, closing doors, going through open doors and gates, all normal things, like getting washed and dressed in the morning, eating, drinking, driving a car, riding a bicycle, going to work, doing the housework, etc., etc. On the other hand, attachments, for example, to material assets, commodities, landscapes, cities, villages, towns, places and the like, but also attachments to people, can become magnets that are again followed by our soul in a life on Earth.

Such multi-layered imprintings leave behind a special engraving on the soul – depending on the person's way of life. Both cosmoses with their planetary constellations, the material macrocosm and the higher macrocosm virtually are the guide, in terms of energy, into those spheres of the beyond that can be the abodes of the soul after disincarnating.

All thinking and acting that cannot be ascribed to the eternal principle, to the absolute law of the All, of equality, freedom, unity, brotherliness and justice, forms the weightiness of the soul and possibly a program for reincarnation. The burdens of the soul are the causes for its person, triggers for the effects, which cause the law of sowing and reaping to become operative. Among others, all behavior patterns against the kingdoms of nature, against the plants and animals, the abuse of the Earth along with all their initiators are recorded, in the material macrocosm as well as in the finer-material macrocosm.

As the result of the energetic accumulation of concentrated energies, an energetic, negative complex develops in the macrocosm. This includes, for example, the crimes against human life, the approval and instigation of wars, as well as the exploitation of the planet Earth and the personal appropriation of the resources of the Earth, through which the rich become ever richer and the poverty and hunger in this world, on the other hand, are more and more rampant. From these concentrated, negative energies, which are violations against the All-law of life, which is unity, so-called matrixes develop. These are the coalescing of same and like energies that are attributed to those people who adopted such wrongdoings as their own.

After the physical death of the person and after a given cosmic order of events, such a soul can make use of this matrix, of its corresponding energetic, like-vibrating cocoon of radiation, to incarnate again, that is, to again take on a body.

Surely many will ask themselves: What is stored in a matrix? When we refer to a matrix, a cocoon of radiation in the material cosmos, this means that a matrix is a body of energy for a possible new incarnation of a soul that is still a human being today. The person predetermines the development of his soul, and after his physical death, it can incarnate again, depending on what the person predetermined. The components that coalesce into a matrix always come from the current person himself. Base behavior patterns, which correspond to the negative content of human feeling, sensing, thinking, speaking and acting, can be "Earth-bound" energies, such as seriously wrong attitudes toward one's fellowman and the planet Earth. An incarnation matrix can develop from this.

And so, the matrix consists of an energetic radiation. In it are stored, for instance, the structure of the new person and all the components of the new body. All organs, all cell systems are energetically recorded. All the organs and cells of the body, all the body's components, whether these function weakly or strongly and healthily in the present person, are registered. The content of the behavior patterns of the respective person are always the pointer on the scale. Since each hair on our head is counted, that is, significant, we can assume that the whole future person in a possible future incarnation of the soul is based on the inputs of the present person.

Every person decides at every moment whether his soul demonstrates an energetically higher quality of life or allocates to itself base degrees of vibration, which, in turn, tend toward the Earth. In all of infinity, nothing happens by chance. We, each and every one of us, are thus, ourselves, the pointer on the scale. It is also not by chance into which family, which circle of fellowmen, the new human being incarnates. He brings with him what he input in previous incarnations as a human being and did not rectify until now.

In the earthly garment, the new person can then decide what he wants to do with his body and his soul. He can continue to weaken his weak organs; but he can also fortify them and bring strength and well-being to his body – again, through the content of his entire behavior.

And so, matrixes are energy fields that magnetically attract souls with the same or like degrees of vibration; a matrix is created through the behavior of the former person. If the person committed grave violations against life, then it will be possible for the soul to incarnate anew by way of the former person's self-made energetic cocoon of radiation, that is, to again live as a human being.

The same holds true for thieves, murderers, criminals and warmongers who have not recognized their guilt and thus, have neither asked for forgiveness nor attained forgiveness by way of making amends. Their souls usually come again with the same drive for action. Without forgiveness and without making amends, the causes continue to exist.

According to the cosmic law, like always is drawn to like; and so, every kind of energy strives, in turn, toward its kind.

Above all, we should be clear about the fact that every wrongdoing that we are aware of from our past or that  is still dormant in us and not yet rectified, that is, cleared up, is registered. As already mentioned, we call this the just law, "the bookkeeping of God, the bookkeeping of the cosmoses."

*Everything is precisely recorded.*
*Therefore, use the moment,*
*use the day!*

To repeat: Nothing, but absolutely nothing, is ever lost. No energy can be extinguished – neither the good, nor the less good, nor the bad.

Every person changes during the course of his life on Earth, in his thinking and speaking, as well as in his doing. All of his behavior is subject to energetic change. Every change in the energetic fabric of forces, which is based on the transformation of energies, be the differential of forces ever so slight – everything is precisely entered in the cosmic bookkeeping either as a debit or credit. Every person and every soul virtually hangs, as it were, on a magnetic rope, on the drip feed of the material macrocosm and of the finer-material cosmos. The cosmic bookkeeping, the bookkeeping of God, doesn't miss the slightest thing. The stars and planets of the material cosmos record the energies; they update and transform energies according to the behavior of every single person.

In all the cosmoses, the same law holds true, also in relation to our behavior toward the world of the animals, plants and minerals, toward the whole Earth: What a person reaps, he will sow.

Nothing is ever lost: Every becoming and passing on the Earth, in and over the Earth, becomes a sediment in the material cosmos. Every readiness to help, but also every act of violence toward people, nature and animals, toward all of the Earth, is precisely recorded and is updated at every instant, according to the "for and against" of the person. We are free today. How do we treat our neighbor? Jesus essentially taught: One should bear the burden of the other; help and serve each other. – When we disparage a person who is weaker than we are, then this content of our thoughts and of our behavior also goes into our soul. With such behavior patterns, we weaken ourselves. This is why Jesus, the Christ, said: *Do to others as you would have them do to you.* Said the other way round: *Do not do to another what you do not want to have done to you.* – We should frequently remind ourselves of this, as well as the rule for life: Use the moment, use the day!

*There is no standstill in infinity.*
*Everything is in motion.*
*Everything is guided and directed*

Everything is guidance, everything is directed. In the three-dimensional world on Earth, there are four seasons, spring, summer, fall and winter, with their varying forms of appearance. How are these respectively arranged? – The material macrocosm is the arbiter of all situations and movements in the three dimensions.

The radiation of the material macrocosm has an effect that goes beyond the immense variety of earthly life forms, including the magnetic currents of the Earth. Via the magnetic currents, animal species are cared for and plant species stimulated. Let us think of the fish, of the migration of whales and eels – how do the animals know that they should be at a certain time and place to reproduce? The sea turtles also always return to the beach where they were born. We also know that carrier pigeons have sensory organs whose function is based on magnetism. On what can migrating birds orient themselves if not on the Earth's magnetic field? There are many, many more examples of this. Here, we can merely indicate a few in order to make clear that we know an abundance of occurrences in nature in which magnetism directs the behavior patterns of living beings.

Native animals also change their coats – who determines and regulates this? In every season, it is thus the material cosmos that tips the scales in manifold ways.

For our understanding: The entire Earth with all its resources – with the nature kingdoms, with the countless ways of life of the animals – is in unity with its Creator and cannot burden itself. And so, it is solely man who violates the All-law of unity, not the world of the animals and plants, not the Mother Earth with all its life forms and resources.

God, the immeasurable All-power, the life, is the ingenious "director," in everyone and in everything – in the smallest as in the largest. In this way, the animals, the plants, the minerals, all individual living organisms, including the microbes, all the colors, forms and fragrances of nature, in their respective designation of consciousness – which emanates from the eternal Creator of the Being – are led and guided by the material macrocosm.

Nowhere in all of infinity is there a standstill. Everything, but really everything – every planet, all the forces of the Being – is inexorably in motion.

Everything that we human beings bring into disorder through our naivety, through our stubbornness, our rashness and egocentricity, what we cause and do that is against the cosmic harmony, that is, against unity, is recorded in the macrocosm, and not lastly, in the finer-material cosmos as a wrongdoing – we also call it sin. It is only the human beings who do mischief and play havoc on the Earth.

Everything is energy. And since no energy is ever lost, it is justly and indestructibly recorded and updated at every moment, thus being in constant movement.

We cannot readily escape the course of communication of the cosmic bookkeeping, the debit and credit – except solely by changing our thinking and making amends.

## *Violations of the cosmic life – and the consequences thereof*

What is a violation of the cosmic life? For example, the deliberate killing of animals, the torture of animals, keeping them in ghettos as slaughter animals, consuming pieces of the carcasses of animals, and much more, all these are against the cosmic life, against the Spirit of Creation.

Everything, but truly everything, that we cause to the planet Earth – for example, cutting down the forests, grinding the stones, redirecting the flow of the waters, constructing dams, building skyscrapers, atomic power plants and other structures – all this is registered in detail by the macrocosms and referred to the individual persons, respectively.

Every shared guilt must be recognized and cleared up. No ifs and buts help. There is no avoidance of this. The path of purification is the path that Jesus taught us: Repent, clear things up, make amends for what can still be amended, and no longer do the same and like things. This path must be very thoroughly and responsibly taken, without limitations; this is also the path of the soul, the path of forgetting.

God does not spoon-feed us or force us. His holy law is love and freedom. We human beings bear within a cosmic soul that is free. We have a mind to weigh and measure with. Thus, in the Spirit of God, we are free beings, responsible for what we do or do not do.

However often a person violates the life – whatever his reason and motivation – everything, but truly everything, has its just and corresponding engraving in the soul as well as in the physical body. As stated, the registry in both macrocosms is precise and just. The cosmic bookkeeping records, among other things, our cravings, our aggressions, but also our readiness to help, and every positive action. All details are energies and are recorded. Nothing is without significance, including every trifle that we talk about, be it ever so small, it is recorded, that is, stored. Absolute justice is done to every person and every soul, through the exact bookkeeping of the cosmoses.

As stated, all forces, all energies, are in constant movement. The All-consciousness, the eternal Intelligence, God, the life, is the movement in all things, that is, the registry, which unceasingly changes with the pros and cons.

Clusters of stars are in the galaxies, in so-called milky ways. Many of these clusters of stars are cosmic magnetic fields, which, among other things, were, and are, formed through group karma. They are energy compounds of like vibration of certain types of people, who, together, for example, endorse wars, who produce armaments and cause wars to be waged; of all those who have their fellowman killed; who force people into slavery and prostitution; who do not fight against the starvation in the world, despite having the possibility to help. In these cosmic magnetic fields, the burdens are recorded of the people who pile up wealth, even though other people are suffering need and illness; who deliberately kill animals or condone and carry out animal experiments; who exploit the Earth; who cut down the trees filled with sap; who violently destroy plant species and much more.

Seen as a whole, all these karmic offences form a group karma. People of this type, depending on their degree of involvement, are even tied into the karma of the world. The individual, energetic correlations of the burdens of each individual person, who is part of the cosmic magnetic fields, of a group karma or world karma, are also recorded in all its details on his soul. And these negative inputs in each soul are in constant movement. The pros and cons at every moment of a human life are very precisely weighed and measured and updated according to their volume of energy. Aside from the soul, the totality of unlawful behavior in all its details is also registered in the corresponding finer-material planetary constellations, where the expiation of the souls occurs, or from where reincarnation takes place via the material cosmos, by way of a matrix, or cocoon.



Every person and every soul is thus a microcosm in the All-macrocosm. The pathways of the human being and the pathways of every single soul are entirely different from those of the others, because each day every person programs himself and his soul in his personal "for and against." For this reason, every person takes his pathway over the heights and through the valleys of his earthly existence, and his soul goes with him. Later, after discarding its physical shell, that is, after its physical death, the soul continues on, to the respective planetary constellations in the material macrocosm, then to the finer-material cosmos, until it finally reaches its home, the Kingdom of God, the absolute, fine-material macrocosm. All things considered, it can be a long cosmic journey. It is also possible for the soul to interrupt its own direct journey, in order to enter a new incarnation and become a new human being.

Every person, every soul has free will. As a result, each person determines his own development according to the behavior patterns that are for or against the eternal cosmic All-law, which is the life, and thus, he also determines the path of development of his soul. All details that are directed against the cosmic law, against the life, burden the soul of the individual, but also his physical body. Depending on the intensity of the burdens, blows of fate, hardship and illness develop from this.

But above all things is the mercy of God. It says, use the moment, use the day and recognize your behavior patterns! Repent and clear them up, make amends for what is still possible and do not commit the same and like things anymore. This applies to the content of all of our feelings, thoughts, words and actions – including all the hurtful desires such as addictions, exploitation, rape, and wanting to take advantage of others.

As already quoted at the beginning, Jesus of Nazareth taught the following:

*Settle matters quickly with your adversary who is taking you to court. Do it while you are still with him on the way, or he may hand you over to the judge, and the judge may hand you over to the officer, and you may be thrown into prison.*

*The transformation of what is
negative and grievous into positive, light
and powerful energies*

We have come to know that everything is energy. Energy is in constant motion and in a state of transformation. When we learn from our wrongdoings and strive to accept the cosmic All-law, the All-consciousness, the Spirit of love, of unity, of freedom and of peace, and monitor ourselves in relation to this, so that we truly take the steps into cosmic freedom, then, in our soul and in us, the person, the following takes place: The negative, the grievous, the burden of negative energies that pull us down, very gradually transforms into positive, light and powerful energies. We become more joyful, happier, and – if it serves the maturity of the soul – healthier. Since every person is the microcosm in the two macrocosms, the same takes place in soul and person.

On this path of transformation of the energy, the soul of the person becomes more light-filled and his physical body also becomes lighter in its vibration. The life on Earth of such a person becomes more balanced; the person becomes more understanding, more approachable and insightful. All in all, this means that the person is on the wavelength of a positive life.

*The unlawfulness that
many people contribute to
forms a group karma*

Let it be said once more: The whole behavior of every person – the content of his thinking and acting, every pro and con, all the details that are for or against his fellow humans and the nature kingdoms – is registered. Everything that is done or not done, among other things, the seriously basic evil, the unlawful, that energetically coincides with people of like mindset, forms, in terms of its severity, a group karma or combines with an already existing group karma of the same type or, depending on the intensity of the guilt, goes into the world karma.

Everything, but really everything, is recorded by the material macrocosm and, at the same time, in all detail for each soul, in the finer-material cosmos – in the planetary constellations to which the soul is energetically allocated, according to the inputs of its human being.

An example to think about more, which seems insignificant to many people, but definitely shows an effect: Whoever cuts down a tree filled with sap for decoration, or for traditional occasions, can be sure he is registered in such karmic fields of group karmas in the macrocosm and in the finer-material cosmos, as well. The severity of it depends on how often and with what intensity each individual offends against the life.

Many people take each day as it comes, without asking themselves: "What do I cause to happen with my behavior?" The majority of people bind themselves to traditions, without thinking much about it. In the registry of the macrocosm, the repeated and traditional over-exploitation of nature is a part of a corresponding group karma, or even of the world karma.

The fewest people know that when they fell a tree, or trees, filled with sap, when they cut them down, the same life forms, the same kind of trees, also experience the suffering of their species, and this, all over the whole Earth. The same is true of the world of animals. The torture and deliberate killing of animals, the slaughter of their bodies, is distressfully perceived by the individuals of this same animal species all over the Earth. The whole extent of this is registered in detail by the macrocosms.

The same applies when animals are cared for, when people love animals, when people provide for animals until their natural death – everything is registered in both macrocosms. And the person who respects nature, who protects it, who sees and pays attention to the life in nature, who cares for nature, is precisely recorded in both macrocosms.

*The finer-material and the
coarse material macrocosms –
their task in the cosmic
course of events*

God is Spirit. An explanation to better understand the word "God," which is attributed by many to the traditional cultural circle of the western world: The Spirit of infinity is the cosmic All-consciousness. Depending on the culture, we human beings call the cosmic All-consciousness either the absolute Intelligence, Allah, Jehovah or the Being. In the western world, the All-Spirit, the Spirit of infinity, is called God. It is always the same Spirit, the same universal, almighty and highest-vibrating power of infinity, the All-consciousness. The Spirit of infinity, the All-consciousness, which is the life in all things, is unity. The All-consciousness, the unending Spirit, which is unity, consists of countless facets of consciousness.

The two macrocosms – the material macrocosm, in which the three-dimensional world is principally recorded, and the finer-material macrocosm, in which the discarnate souls live according to their state of consciousness – are merely the spheres of the Fall, which will be inhaled by the eternal All-consciousness, according to temporal processes. In this process, they will be transformed into fine-material energies and again integrated into the eternally existing Kingdom of God, the absolute macrocosm. From the Kingdom of God, fine-material part-planets were given by God to the rebellious divine beings to take with them; over unimaginable periods of time these part-planets have formed into the finer-material macrocosm and the coarse-material macrocosm, so that the rebellious beings would have a conditional dwelling place. Both macrocosms – the finer-material and the coarse-material – are therefore merely temporary.

The material cosmos is the registry for the three-dimensional world – a world, which Fall-beings and human beings created by turning away from God. As stated, in the material macrocosm, the so-called matrixes are found, energetic cocoons, for a possible new incarnation of a soul, so that this soul, as a human being, again finds the conditions of life on Earth that correspond to it in the three-dimensional world. This alternation of coming and going lies within the free will of the human being.

## The all-encompassing work of the eternal Spirit, of the cosmic All-consciousness

The cosmic All-consciousness is the Spirit of unity. As mentioned, it is active not only in all plant species, in every animal, in every tiny, inconspicuous living being, for example, in the microbes – everywhere, the All-Spirit, the All-consciousness, is present. The substances of all minerals are also a part of the All-consciousness. Everything, but truly everything, contains the unending, everlasting life, which is the All-consciousness, and in which a continual evolution is at work. There is nothing that does not bear in itself the All-consciousness. Every atom, every molecule, the smallest component of the All, is a bearer of the All-consciousness, a bearer of the eternally effective life.

All people and souls are part of the All-consciousness, the life. In the Kingdom of God, on the other hand, all pure beings are compressed All-consciousness; their spiritual body is divine, but they themselves are not God. The difference between being a part of it, that is, of *belonging* to the All-consciousness, and of *being* compressed All-consciousness, is the following – which I repeat:

The material cosmos and the finer-material cosmos are both energies that have been transformed down, they are split-offs from the Kingdom of God. Both cosmoses are – as stated – only temporary. They serve the human beings and the souls, those beings that have turned away from the All-consciousness, from God. This turning away from God is also called sin.

The nature kingdoms, all the minerals, all the forces of the Earth, like animals, plants, minerals, etc., are not burdened. They were given to human beings for understanding, realization and for turning back and changing their ways, so that the people could find their way from egocentricity to the unity that is God, because all life belongs to the divine unity. In the very basis of his soul, the human being is part of the one root, the unity in God. In the very basis of his soul, the person is not from this world; his true being comes from the Kingdom of God, the All-consciousness GOD, the eternal Intelligence; and at some point in time, it will return again to its infinitely eternal roots of love, of unity, of peace and of freedom.

And even if it is still such a very long way for the soul – it will, as all will, go the path of the purification of its guilt and through this, the path of forgetting, so that in the end, as a spirit being, it is again in the eternal Father's house, with God, its Father.

Unfortunately, most people have not yet come to understand that they burden themselves, and thus, their soul, when they violate the unity, which is the life in God, that is, when they offend against people, against the cosmic unity, the nature kingdoms, the whole Earth.

Whoever thinks and acts against the life sins against the All-consciousness, the All-law, the Spirit of freedom, of unity – that is, he offends against the life.

Many people are under the spell of science. But, in what way? Many are of the opinion that science must know the cosmic correlations. Scientists research and research, but until now, they have not yet fathomed the All-Intelligence, the All-consciousness. They talk, for example, of the so-called "black holes" in the material cosmos and know that the "black holes" attract whole solar systems and that in them the energies are transformed – but the why and what for remain unanswered.

The All-consciousness is the creating power, it is the Creator, who is also incessantly active in entire spheres of the Fall, transforming energies, that is, reshaping them, for the benefit of the eternal Being, to which all of infinity belongs. With reference to the law of energetic transformation, the black holes can readily be described as cosmic "sorting machines," which transform the energies of planet parts and even solar systems and then allocate them to the corresponding cosmos. These energies then go again  into the coarse-material macrocosm, or into the finer cosmos, depending on whether the life on Earth continues to spread or whether it can be led back into the infinitely eternal law, into the All-consciousness.

For example, if many animal species die or even die out and the same species does not appear again on the Earth, then stars and planets of the material macrocosm are attracted by the black holes and transformed into finer, energetic substances. Such changes in the material macrocosm are what we human beings call the "dying" of suns and planets. However, we cannot talk about "dying" in a negative sense. Nothing disappears from the great spectrum of life forms at the drop of a hat. Nothing dissolves into nothing. There is absolutely no such thing as "nothing"! It is a "dying" in the following sense: It ceases to be in one form, in order to become another, higher form of being: more radiant, shining, approaching its spiritual origin.

The black holes thus magnetically attract those stars and planets that need to be transformed, because, for example, animal species are withdrawing from the Earth.

Negative inputs from former human beings are also energetically transformed, because their souls have developed higher on the path of purification and of forgetting. In this way, too, stars and planets are transformed and led to higher consciousness.

The creating Spirit, the All-consciousness, is untiringly active. He is effective in the finer-material cosmos, where the souls are located. He is active in, on and over the Earth and in the material macrocosm. He is the helmsman of the forces; He is the transformer of energies into finer-material substances, into fine-material forces – or, even into coarser substances again, which He then allocates to the material macrocosm. This takes place, among other things, when souls incarnate or when individual nature genera again appear on the Earth, as, for example, animal or plant species.

The development of awareness in greater contexts of meaning is called for; this is the reason for repetition. Whether the human being on Earth merely endorses formations and traditions, or whether he is a party to them, whether he takes profit from projects that are against the Earth with all its life forms and resources, and how much – everything, but really everything, is weighed, measured and recorded according to the activity of the individual.

Dear readers, still many things, infinitely many things, could be said about the cosmic bookkeeping, the just registry of the All-consciousness. On the topic of "The Human Being, the Microcosm in the Macrocosm" and on "the soul in the purification planes," even if whole series of bookshelves were filled with details on the debit and credit sides, with the absolute justice of the All-consciousness – it would not be possible to pass on everything.

*The path of forgetting –*
*The path back*
*to the eternal heavenly homeland*
*for every soul*

Let us engross ourselves more deeply in the topic of "The Path of Forgetting." The path of forgetting is the path to the everlasting, seven-dimensional Kingdom of God, to our eternal homeland, to the eternal, primordial roots of the divine being that pulses in the very basis of each soul. No matter how often and for how long we may walk the path of forgetting – the soul, via the planetary constellations of the finer-material macrocosm or the human being in further incarnations – the path is given, because no energy is ever lost. We cannot bring to mind often enough the fact that our divine body in the very basis of our soul is eternal, cosmic energy from the Kingdom of God; for this reason, no soul will ever be lost.

The path of forgetting is conveyed only by using simple words, because it is the path to the seven-dimensional eternal kingdom, the eternal fine-material macrocosm, which cannot be described in detail by using our three-dimensional words and terms. In the life on Earth of human beings, everything is subject to the limitations of three dimensions, including our language. For this reason, what happened through the Fall-thoughts, by splitting off from the Kingdom of God, will be given in simple language, insofar as it is possible to understand it. Any scientific embossing and mathematical formulas would only bring more confusion into the description of the great event, which, as stated, can only be implied with three-dimensional words. God is a just God. As long as the Fall exists, His power of creation is concerned with support and help for His still-burdened children and with the transformation of the finer-material macrocosm and of the material macrocosm, for these energies belong to the Kingdom of God, the absolute macrocosm.

As already mentioned, we people forget a lot in terms of our past. But not all of it has been paid off, annulled and transformed into higher forces, even if we can no longer remember it or don't want to remember it. Often, we don't want to believe or face what burdens our soul and body in connection to people, nature, animals and minerals, to all of the Earth.

The human being is shaped by the three-dimensional, that's just the way it is. His soul, on the other hand, is finer-material. It is surrounded by the dimension that it radiates according to the behavior of its person. For this reason, it is not visible to the person, neither in an incarnate nor discarnate state. What the soul has stored by way of the behavior of its person, cannot simply be cast off by the person and dismissed by deliberately forgetting; he cannot undo it.

After the death of our body, our soul takes with it the positive as well as the negative aspects that have not been cleared up, that corresponded to its development as a human being. Whether the former person forgot or wanted to forget, or whether he no longer remembers, doesn't make a difference – recorded is recorded.

_The path of the soul after
the demise of its physical body_

According to the natural law, the material body belongs to the Earth. At the moment the body passes away, the soul very gradually detaches itself from the mortal shell, the body, and immediately belongs to another aggregate consciousness, a dimension that is appropriate to it.

The connection to people – who were very close to the one who has now passed on, who lived with him for many years, who acquired some things together with that person in the temporal and built some things for their families or acquaintances, which were of value to them – can become a problem for the person who has now died.

Those who remain behind do not see the soul of the person they were close to. However, conversely, the soul sees the people with whom it lived and was active, because the same magnet, whether human being or soul, attracts the same aspects again and again. During the initial time after the physical death of the person, his soul still finds itself among those who were close to it. It still lives in the notion of its value as a human being in all that brought the human being a sense of home, security, gain, prestige and the like, that is, what was meaningful to the person. The soul of this person cannot simply disengage; the magnetism to the values of external things is too strong. The magnet is the surroundings in which the former person felt well, where he nurtured his habits, where he was well regarded, where he had his possessions, made profit, etc., etc. If it cannot simply disengage itself from this, despite the knowledge that it is now a soul, then it remains invisible in its familiar earthly surroundings, invisible to the human eye.

At first, it refuses to believe the impulses that reach it in terms of its further development as a soul, because they stimulate in it many things that have not been overcome, which, as a human being, it wanted to forget or forgot. The inputs in the material macrocosm become ever clearer in the soul. The forgotten becomes visible in different sequences of pictures that indicate to the soul that it rectify the negativity that is again current and recognizable in its feelings and sensations, that is, that it clear them up, detach itself from them and then be able to forget them.

All the suffering, the sorrow and the pain, which we have caused to our fellowman through our egoism or indifference, comes alive in these picture sequences. Since these pictures are the engraving in our soul, we cannot simply shake them off; instead, we will experience them on our own soul body. Pain, grief, loneliness, being forsaken, suffering and worry that others had to experience because of us, we will endure and suffer as a soul on our soul body. This is why Jesus the Nazarene taught the following, and we repeat:

*Settle matters quickly with your adversary who is taking you to court. Do it while you are still with him on the way, or he may hand you over to the judge, and the judge may hand you over to the officer, and you may be thrown into prison.*

Beyond the sending consciousness of the coarse material macrocosm, a finer-material planetary constellation from the finer-material macrocosm gives, in the form of energy, hints to the soul regarding the path to its further place of destination.

If we human beings become aware of the fact that every person dies for himself alone and that each one goes the path of forgetting alone, then it is much easier for us to understand that each one of us is a specific individual who surrounds himself with the energies of his own personal inputs. This is his aura, here, as a human being, and in the beyond, as a soul.

Each person has his own specific daily routine with its individual character. Everything that goes on during the day, all the variations of behavior of the person are followed by the material macrocosm. The whole scale of needs, all habits and mannerisms, are energies, often registered in the macrocosm as a concentrated collective of like energies.

No energy is ever lost. All these personal things and customs, which, in the end, are a part of each individual person, are recorded by the material macrocosm. Even when these traits, which automatically are a part of existence in our three-dimensional world, don't burden us, they are nevertheless a part of the path of forgetting.

Everything that we accomplish as a matter of course each day, because life on Earth simply requires this, the discarnate soul doesn't need anymore. It lives in another dimension, which is finer-material. But it retains the habits for a long time, because every action is energy.

To elucidate, I repeat:

Everything that is part of being a human being – a part of the three-dimensional world – even if it is not a burden for the soul, is nevertheless taken into the other world, into the beyond. Even those things that don't burden it have to be discarded on the path of forgetting.

However, everything that is burdensome for the soul is recorded by the planetary constellations of the finer-material macrocosm. Substantial burdens caused by the person can be a grievous engraving in his soul and, as already mentioned, can also form in the material macrocosm as a so-called matrix, also called a cocoon. Through this, a very heavily burdened soul is given the possibility to incarnate again. It will feel the urge for this if it cannot let go of its previous actions as a human being and wants to live as a human being again.

And when two people procreate a child – a man and a woman, who have a similar radiation as the engraving of the aforementioned soul – the soul will do everything it can to be with these parents as a newborn human child. There are no coincidences. The same and like things attract each other.

## *A discarnate soul,*
## *bound to its former surroundings*

So, nothing happens by chance! Everything is guided; everything is directed; everything comes into movement at the right time and is manifest sooner or later. Many a soul that has tied itself to the temporal as a human being has great difficulty, for example, to disconnect itself from places, countries, money and possessions. The surroundings, which were agreeable and useful to its former person, bind many a soul. Sensitive people notice the presence of the soul of a person who died shortly before.

Often, there are reports that the deceased mother – or father, grandfather, grandmother, or even, when a child has died in the family – is still nearby, to be sure, invisible, but tangibly present. People of less sensitivity, people who affirm this world as the sole reality, will dismiss such feelings of perception as maudlin sentimentality or a figment of the imagination.

It is conceivable that many a soul can disengage itself from its customary surroundings only with great difficulty, if, as a human being, it was surrounded by great wealth, by an extravagant lifestyle, by festivities and luxury, if it lived in beautiful landscapes, if it acquired prestige through its possessions and much more. Everything that a person considers as his own and that he has tied to himself is for such a soul an impediment to separate itself from this binding style of life.

If the soul cannot detach itself from its surroundings, then it may, perhaps, continue to live among the people with whom it had lived and enjoyed its life as a human being in abundance and wealth. It tries to include itself in the conversations of its intimates, but it isn't heard or perceived. For such a soul, this is not only very painful and inacceptable; these situations often stimulate it to incarnate again, to become a human being again.

Another, similar example: A sensitive person who was very close to a deceased person feels a shiver running up his spine every now and then, and he thinks: "The soul of the father who recently died is still here; it listens and participates in the conversations." The impression cannot be wiped away and this person says: "I feel it quite clearly." – Why does this person feel a shiver along his spine? Because the soul present touched this person; it wants to convey something, to establish communication.

The shiver that many a person feels is the radiation of the finer-material body, of the soul, the aura, which surrounds the soul. The radiation of the soul is much cooler than the radiation of the body, and this is why the brief shiver along the spine, with its neural pathways.

Regardless of the milieu in which the former human being grew up and lived, the soul mostly remains at this place for a certain period of time and tries to continue to live as usual in its previous circle of activity as a human being. Not seldom, a soul has to painfully recognize via the irradiation of the macrocosm that it is no longer perceived by its former friends, by its family. The material macrocosm acts upon the soul as an intensity of radiation and tries to help it realize its situation. The soul has to eventually realize that the surroundings, which it had once grown to love, are no longer available to it and that now, very gradually, and via its inputs, it has to follow the path that the person predetermined for it through his behavior. Through the radiation, it is stimulated to follow the path of forgetting via the material macrocosm into a corresponding plane of purification, to the planetary constellation of like vibration.

Once the soul has grasped what it is all about, it gradually feels the pull to other life situations, that is, to inputs of its life, to its active inputs, and begins to turn away from its former surroundings as a human being, following the path of forgetting step by step. In doing so, much of which was once so meaningful will become unimportant to it. Among other things, the path of forgetting means to very gradually – often with great difficulty – detach oneself from those things which gave the soul as a human being security and a hold on life. Slowly, very slowly, the soul dissociates itself from its previous circle of activity as a human being. It follows the path, shown to it by the material macrocosm and a planetary constellation in the finer-material cosmos.

A soul that has learned to interpret the radiation and guidance of both cosmoses begins to let go, even when the longing for its former life on Earth still draws it bindingly. But its realization, be it ever so bitter, is then its path, the path of forgetting, so that, in another dimension, it may remedy what still adheres to it. The soul gradually lets go of the feelings of warmth and coldness, of sleeping and awakening, of familiar objects, of beautiful landscapes, of a luxurious life, of feudal eating and drinking habits, also, for example, of the comfortable chair it had grown to love as a human being, in which its person sat hours upon hours, enjoying the view of the idyllic landscape.

To all intents and purposes, every person and every soul has to find and take up in itself the path to its origin by fulfilling the laws of infinity.

To repeat: As soon as the soul withdraws from the needs and customs of its former person, from its habits and luxurious life, the forgetting begins. The sensitive person then notices that the soul is no longer nearby. Once the soul follows the path of forgetting, other memories will awaken in it. These are aspects of wrong attitudes that are a part of the engraving in its soul, and which, on this, its temporary destination, it should recognize, repent of and discard in a finer-material planetary constellation.

On the path of forgetting to a finer-material planetary constellation, further tasks of purification are stimulated, which the soul carries as an engraving. On its path, its body radiation also changes. The soul takes on other facial features. It wears a finer-material soul garment, an ethereal garment, which, in its nuances of color, corresponds to the radiation consciousness of the soul and to the planetary constellation in the beyond allotted to it.

## "The Life that I Chose Myself"

The path of another soul can be the following: Perhaps the former person who is now deceased created a matrix in the material cosmos via its soul, to perhaps reincarnate as quickly as possible. The lawful interrelationships are explained to the soul and the indication is given to it that repeated incarnations are not the will of God. Higher beings show the soul, which is pressing toward a new physical birth, its engraving, its present wrong attitudes against the life of unity, of freedom, of the love for God and neighbor, so that already in the beyond, it may recognize these, repent of them and clear them up.

Many a soul doesn't want this, because its matrix is emitting its once wrong human attitudes to it, that is, the matrix is bringing them into movement. Then, despite the teaching, the unregenerate soul may figure on the possibility to again acquire a new body on Earth.

Light-filled beings, which accompany it, will show the soul the important aspects of its existence as the new human being, that is, what would be in store for it, in case it were to incarnate again.

A poem, attributed to Hermann Hesse, can be helpful to us so that we recognize that the soul is never alone, that it is always taught, that it is always guided, that something always comes into movement in it. The poem is called:

## "The Life that I Chose Myself"

Before I came into this earthly life,
I was shown how I would live it.
There were troubles; there was grief,
There was misery and the burden of suffering.
There was the vice that was to seize me,
There was the delusion  that captivated me.
There was the quick rage, in which I rampaged,
There was hatred, arrogance, pride and shame.

But there were also the joys of those days
Filled with light and beautiful dreams,
Where neither lamentation nor vexation exist,
And everywhere the fount of gifts flows free.

Where love gives the bliss of letting go
To the one still bound in the garment of earth.
Where the one who escaped human pain
Thinks high thoughts as though a chosen one.

I was shown the bad and the good,
I was shown the fullness of my failings,
I was shown the wounds that ran with blood,
I was shown the angels' helping deed.
And as I so beheld my life to come,
I heard a being ask the question:
If I dare to live this life,
For the hour of decision was at hand.

So once more I weighed all the bad.
"This is the life I want to live,"
My answer resounded strong and decided,
And I quietly took on my new fate.
And so, I was born into this world,
So it was as I entered a new life.
I don't lament when often I'm not glad,
For I affirmed it when not yet born.


From the words of the poem, we can see
that before a new incarnation, as souls we are

always thoroughly instructed about what to expect in a life on Earth, that is, what our starting position or what certain constellations in the earthly existence will be, our predispositions, etc., etc. What we do with this, whether we develop positively or not from this, lies in the freedom of every single one of us.

*The spiritual structure of
the fine-material body of divine beings.
The spirit body burdened
by unlawful energies – the soul*

We've already heard about divine beings, whose fine-material body is called a spirit being. It is made up of a particle structure, as opposed to our physical body, which consists of cells, bones, tendons, ligaments, nerves, etc.

The divine body is an absolutely flexible structure, through which radiates the immeasurable primordial power, the law of the eternal Being, the All-consciousness. To imagine the particle structure, the scales on a fish can serve as a comparison. The particles of the divine body lie like scales, row upon row, next to, and over, each other. Each particle is permeated by the light of the universe, the All-consciousness, the law of the Kingdom of God that is omnipresent. The spiritual, divine body unceasingly receives the primordial radiation of the Being via the divine core of being, which is the heart of the spirit body.

The primordial power of the Being, the cosmic All-consciousness, consists of seven primordial basic powers. Because God is unity, each radiation of the primordial power is contained in all the others. Consequently, the seven primordial powers radiate in seven-times-seven facets into infinity and, among other things, are effective in all the particles of the spiritual body, as well as in each step of evolution in the consciousness of the different forms of life. For this reason, each particle is filled by the cosmic All-consciousness, the light of infinity.

The mentality of a spirit being – we human beings would speak about specific abilities – can be recognized in its radiation, which is related to one basic power, respectively. The mentality, which corresponds to one of the seven basic powers of God – Order, Will, Wisdom, Earnestness, Patience, the same as Kindness, Love or Mercy, the same as Gentleness – shapes, as stated, the particle structure of the divine body and is expressed in the nature of the spirit being's garments.

We know from the divine world that within every person dwells a soul, whose origin is divine and whose eternal homeland is the Kingdom of God. After the death of its body, our soul sojourns in the finer-material spheres of the beyond. The soul, like the spirit body of the heavenly beings, is also made up of a particle structure; however, the particles of the soul are shadowed. The radiation of a soul corresponds to its burdens, which its former human being imposed on it through his unlawful behavior against the cosmic All-law of love for God and neighbor. We human beings call the thinking and acting against God "sin." And so, the sins that the person committed and has not yet expiated, went into the corresponding particles of the soul as a shadowing. The result of this is that as long as our original, divine body is burdened by us human beings, it is called the soul.

According to the radiation of the soul – also described as the aura or corona – it wears its soul garments. It is what surrounds the soul, what it bears as burdens and thus, reflects. It is its momentary active aura. The various color nuances that indicate the nature of its burdens are called the soul garments; their vibration is like their radiation. It is its present energetic garment, which envelops it.

## *The pathways of the soul*

Just as the person is on a journey, so is the soul on a journey, as well. It, too, always has the choice of which path it wants to take. Either it strives to return soon to the eternal homeland, the fine-material macrocosm, the Kingdom of God, or it remains for a certain time as soul in a purification plane that corresponds to its radiation intensity. Likewise, it is also free to incarnate again. No matter for which of these possibilities the soul decides, it is always enveloped by what its person once imposed on it and that has not yet been cleared up, the guilt that has not yet been paid off.

Every state of consciousness of the soul is its momentary condition. This is also visible on its soul garment and when it reincarnates, that is, becomes a human being, it is in him as the radiation of his soul. It brings along into its incarnation its positive as well as its negative sides. During the development of its new earthly existence, some of this will become active. It successively comes into effect once the young person is able to discern between good and bad.

The development of a discarnate soul can be the following: If the soul has largely rectified, that is, cleared up, the negative features that cling to it, its characteristics that were not good and that corresponded to the image of its former person, then the next steps follow, as appropriate, to further, perhaps even higher, more light-filled planetary constellations. The soul perceives the respective frequencies in its current consciousness. Its present abode corresponds to its state of consciousness. It is stimulated to look at what still clings to it as burdensome, in order to rectify it.

On this further pathway of the soul, it must often painfully recognize on its soul body what its engraving is clearly pointing out to it, for example, offences against people, the torture of animals, the wanton killing of animals, the consumption of animal flesh. Also the defilement of nature and the exploitation of the Earth are pictorially recorded in the soul of the so-called sinner, the former person, and are often connected with suffering and pain. What it caused as a person to people, animals, to the entire Mother Earth, be it torment, pain, suffering and much more, it now has to bear and to feel on its own body. This is the so-called expiation.

If the soul becomes aware of such and similar burdens, then it will be taught anew about this by light-filled beings – just as it is always taught on its pathway. Its garment of consciousness unfolds itself from the soul, for every radiation, whether positive or negative, has its specific color and form that fits the radiation of the soul. On its pathway, the next step becomes visible, that which should be cleared up by it. This becomes visible in the soul body, the soul garment.

On all the soul's pathways, the appearance of the soul body and of the soul garments change.

The more the soul develops spiritually, the more comprehensively it recognizes its engraving, repents of it and clears it up, often expiating it painfully, the more the finer-material body structure changes, through the transformation of energy, from the negative to the positive. The finer-material body becomes brighter; the soul garments become more light-filled, the facial features nobler. Step by step, the soul-being approaches its true, eternal homeland. Very gradually, its divine nature, the fine-material spirit being, unfolds itself.

And so, it totally depends on the soul in terms of how it decides. If it follows the higher insight to continue to develop spiritually by following the path that continues to recognize and clear up its guilt, then the base, the guilt, will be transformed by the All-consciousness and it will reach a higher intensity of light. What is no longer present in terms of sin, or guilt, is thus paid off and, with this, forgotten.

On the other hand, if the soul wants to incarnate, then it goes into the depths again.

Once more, it approaches the material macrocosm, in order to then become a new human being, as soon as possible. Every human being, every soul, has the free will to decide freely. If the soul returns to another incarnation as a human being, then – as stated – it will go via the matrixes, which its former person created. Inherent to reincarnation is the fact that the person is no longer aware of the human turbulences of past incarnations, that is, they are "forgotten." But in this case, of course, no step has been taken on the aforesaid path of forgetting – through this, soul and person do not leave the sins behind them. At some point or other, the corresponding guilt will be pointed out by the law of the deed, the law of sowing and reaping. The path of forgetting now becomes the path of disclosure.

*A soul incarnates – Person and soul
are measured by the divine principles
of the Ten Commandments and
the Sermon on the Mount of Jesus*

What does an incarnation look like? A child is born. What this soul experienced in the material macrocosm and, perhaps, in finer-material planetary constellations and what it brings with it from previous incarnations – both the positive and the negative – is, at first, no longer tangible; it is "forgotten." The child grows up. As stated, once it has learned to discern between good and bad – that is, after a number of corresponding years on Earth – many a thing from previous incarnations comes into effect, which now this person should rectify, step by step.

We know the Ten Commandments of God through Moses and the Sermon on the Mount of Jesus of Nazareth. Taken together, they constitute the life, and are given to every single person as the path to the Father's house. The life is eternal and, therefore, it is not here and there. The life is unity; it is the cosmic life, the cosmic law, which is expressed in the following principles: Equality, Freedom, Unity, Brotherliness and Justice. These All-principles, lived – which are ultimately the path home to the eternal Being – are disregarded by most people. But the person and his soul, which are and remain wayfarers until they immerse in the mighty ocean of the All-One, in the law of unity, will be measured by these divine principles, which symbolize the unity; the deeds of the individual will also be weighed accordingly. This is the truth, which we can also deduce from the following parable:

*Now a man came up to Jesus and asked, Teacher, what good thing must I do to get eternal life? Why do you ask me about what is good? Jesus replied. There is only One who is good. If you want to enter life, obey the commandments. Which ones? the man enquired. Jesus replied, Do not kill, do not commit adultery, do not steal, do not give false testimony, honor your father and mother, and love your neighbor as yourself. All these I have kept, the young man said. What do I still lack?*

*Jesus answered, If you want to be perfect, go, sell your possessions and give to the poor, and you will have treasure in heaven. Then come, follow me. When the young man heard this, he went away sad, because he had great wealth. Then Jesus said to his disciples, I tell you the truth, it is hard for a rich man to enter the kingdom of heaven. Again I tell you, it is easier for a camel to go through the eye of a needle than for a rich man to enter the kingdom of God.*

In our world there have always been many rich people, and today, there are ever more rich people, and because of this, there are also many souls that tend toward the Earth again and again, because their matrixes, their radiation cocoons, are programmed accordingly. A soul that cannot separate itself from its money and property, from prestige and wealth, always nourishes the hope of being able to incarnate again into this oasis of "feeling comfortable." The soul that belongs to such a clan of money and property strives over and over again to incarnate into a so-called "long-standing, well-to-do" family clan.

By way of marriage and the procreation of children, many a one from the family clan creates a cradle for a soul that is shaped this way, so that as a human being it can again be where the former person was in a previous incarnation, in surroundings that still are the soul's one and all. But at some point in time, the cradle for such a soul that is caught up in its world of desires will remain empty or a distant soul will help itself to this cradle, that is, it will incarnate, and it will have no connection to this great wealth. The person, whose soul brings with it no sense of value for this wealth, can accept the huge inheritance or lead it into chaos. Or a time of upheaval will take from the person the chance to preserve the wealth or even to increase it.

In the temporal, there is nothing eternal nor does eternity exist. No wealth exists eternally. The ravages of time do not gnaw solely on the rich and on wealth. At some point in time, it is over: The ravages of time will lead the magnificent, the "comfortable oases," the money and assets, into "once upon a time." No Earth-bound soul can maintain the wealth of its former human being and claim it for itself over and over again by incarnating into the same clan. At some point in time, the person will suffer and, after shedding its body, his soul will suffer, as well. At some point in time, it will have had enough of being a person of power.

Every person has his individual path of life to follow, and every soul continues to deliver itself up to this for so long until it realizes what life means, and that without "forgetting" the human things and pleasures, there is no path of liberation, and certainly not without overcoming, repenting and making amends for wrong attitudes against the law of unity.

What we as a human being have forgotten or has been transformed in our "soul-computer" depends entirely upon whether it was only general needs or general habits within the course of the three-dimensional, or whether, as stated, there were wrong attitudes, that is, sinfulness, against the life.

The following is advisable, as a help towards self-help: Look at those things that occupy us on a daily basis, the occurrences and situations, the striving for power and practice of power, from a somewhat greater distance. Above all, this applies to the personal aspects of the individual himself and not to another person.

## The path home to the eternal Being of every soul, of every human being, with the Christ of God

The word that leads to life is the path of truth. There is only one truth, which is God, and God is without limits. In the origin of our soul, we are divine beings, that is, spirit beings, which are bound neither to time nor space. Every spirit being is practically an equal heir to the Kingdom of God and thus, free, without limits or reservations. The spirit body of the divine being is compressed, eternal law; for this reason, it is divine, but not God. Every divine being freely moves in the All, in the cosmos, and so, it is independent, because it personifies the law of life. It lives in the All-principle: Equality, Freedom, Unity, Brotherliness, the same as Brotherli- Sisterliness, and Justice, from which results, among other things, the limitless sending and receiving, the unending cosmic All-communication. The eternally pure Being is the law of infinity. It is the pathways of the spirit beings on which they move. We human beings would say – coined to fit the reality of Earth – they are our roads and pathways.

It becomes ever clearer that there are no limits for the divine beings – in God, their Creator and eternal Father, they are boundless spirit beings in the eternal Being. The path to the eternal Being is the path of every soul and human being. The sooner we walk it, the more quickly we will be in the eternal homeland: divine beings, pure, eternal Being, compressed, eternal All-law. Each person, each soul, itself, determines when and with how many hurdles we will take this path to the boundless unity. God is the freedom; He does not decide for us.

So that we human beings may recognize God's love and freedom, the Eternal, our heavenly Father, gave us the Ten Commandments through Moses, which are excerpts from the eternal law of freedom. Mind you, they say "you shall" and not "you must." It is in this that lies the freedom of every single being. Freedom is a heavenly property, which is rooted in God's love. It says:

*You shall love the Lord, your God with all your heart and with all your soul and with all your mind and with all your strength. This is the greatest and first commandment. The second is this: You shall love your neighbor as yourself.*

True freedom brings equality and peace. True peace brings unity, and unity contains brotherliness, the same as brotherli- sisterliness. The brotherliness, which is the same as brotherli- sisterliness, also contains justice, because before the countenance of God, all His children are equal. This is the path to the Kingdom of God, and there is no other way.

Dear fellow people, each one of us has a unique treasure in his soul, a wonderful guide and companion: It is the Spirit of the Christ of God, the Redeemer-light, which shines on our way via the material cosmos, via the finer-material cosmos, until we immerse into the mighty ocean, God, into the All-law of the eternal Being, and are again eternally at home in the eternal mansions, which Jesus of Nazareth announced with the following words:

*In my Father's house are many mansions; if it were not so, would I have told you, "I go to prepare a place for you"?*

Let us wish one another a secure path to the eternal Father's house!

*Gabriele*

## *Epilog*

The path of forgetting sheds new light on the significance of our days on Earth. Nothing, from what we have to answer for, should be overlooked. It is only once we have completely nullified, that is, undone, our indebtedness by way of self-recognition and purification, will it then totally and completely be relegated to that which is forgotten. For then, the Christ of God has transformed all the bad into light-filled, fine-material energy forms.

In this process, we are not spared the painstaking work of monitoring ourselves and working things off. Note well – it is about being allowed to forget! To accomplish this in the right way is where our personal responsibility lies toward the life and the Universal Spirit, our heavenly Father.

These cosmic processes make every hour, every minute of our life on Earth profoundly invaluable to us!

# Read also ...

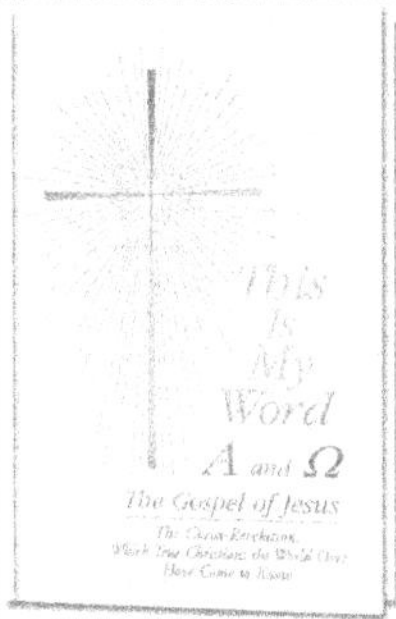

## This Is My Word
### A and Ω

*The Gospel of Jesus*
*The Christ-Revelation,*
*which True Christians*
*the World Over*
*Have Come to Know*

Much of what Jesus taught was kept hidden from the people, for in today's Bible there is only what Jerome (4th century AD) was allowed to take into the Bible. In the divine work of revelation "This Is My Word" we read from Christ himself the truth about His life, His thinking and work as Jesus of Nazareth.

**From the Contents**: Childhood and Youth of Jesus - The Falsification of the Teachings of Jesus of Nazareth - Pharisees, Yesterday and Today - Jesus Loved the Animals and Always Championed them - The Sermon on the Mount - Meaning and Purpose of Life on Earth - Prerequisites for Healing the Body - On the Nature of God - God Does Not Rage or Punish. The Law of Cause and Effect - The Teaching of "Eternal Damnation" is a Mockery of God - About Death, Reincarnation and Life - Equality of Men and Women - The Comming Time and the Future of Mankind - The True Meaning of the Deed of Redemption of Christ, and much more...

1094 pps., softcover, Order No. S 007en,
ISBN: 978-1-890841-38-6, $15.00,

# The Speaking All-Unity

## The Word of the Universal Creator-Spirit

### A Cosmic Work of Teaching and Learning from the School of Divine Wisdom

Taken from conversations with Gabriele, compiled by Martin Kübli and Ulrich Seifert

Have you always had the feeling of being connected to a higher power, but not to any religion? Because the teachings were inconsistent, because your questions were not answered or because the religious words and the deeds did not appear to be in accord?

This books will make it possible for you to develop a new image of God. From the Big Bang to the question of why there are addictions, murder and natural disasters, you will find answers to the questions which denominational teachings leave unanswered.

Learn why the respectful and loving treatment of other beings of life is so important, about what we can learn from the animals and how we can live in harmony with nature. And, find out how you, too, can develop a more conscious life: with knowledge, a respectful and loving way of seeing things, meditations, and practice.

**Includes an Audio-CD with two meditations:**

**1. "Everything Is in Bloom" – a meditative virtual walk**

**2. "Our True Being" – a meditative cosmic view**

382 pp., hardbd., many fotos, Order No. S173en
ISBN:978-1-890841-33-1, $ 29.00

We will be happy to send you our free catalog
Gabriele Publishing House,
ax-Braun-Str. 2, 97828 Marktheidenfeld, Germany
info@gabriele-publishing-house.com